Explore new ideas!

W...
Friends and Family

Read exciting literature, science and social studies texts!

Become an expert writer!

Build vocabulary and knowledge to unlock the Wonders of reading!

 Use your student login to explore your interactive Reading/Writing Workshop, practice close reading, and more.

Go Digital! **www.connected.mcgraw-hill.com**

Cover and Title Pages: Nathan Love

www.mheonline.com/readingwonders

Send all inquiries to:
McGraw-Hill Education
Two Penn Plaza
New York, NY 10121

ISBN: 978-0-07-898074-9
MHID: 0-07-898074-7

Printed in the United States of America.

1 2 3 4 5 6 7 8 9 LWI 22 21 20 19 18 17   A

Wonders

An English Language Arts Program

Program Authors

Diane August

Donald R. Bear

Janice A. Dole

Jana Echevarria

Douglas Fisher

David Francis

Vicki Gibson

Jan Hasbrouck

Margaret Kilgo

Jay McTighe

Scott G. Paris

Timothy Shanahan

Josefina V. Tinajero

Mc Graw Hill Education

Unlock the
Wonders
of
Reading

With your *Reading/Writing Workshop* you will:

- Closely read and reread literature and informational text

- Discuss what you have read with your peers

- Become a better writer and researcher

- Look for text evidence as you respond to complex text

Get Ready to Become:

- Lifelong Learners
- Critical Thinkers
- Part of the Community of Learning

READ and REREAD

Exciting Literature

Fables, folktales, and fantasies will take you to new worlds. Through stories and poems discover new wonders. It's all waiting for you!

Informational Texts

Read about amazing people and brave heroes. Informational text will open up the worlds of Science and Social Studies.

ACT
Access Complex Text

As you read, take notes on what you don't understand. Look at the questions below. They will help you move in the right direction.

VOCABULARY

What can I do if I come across a word I don't know? I can look for context clues or look up the word in a dictionary.

MAKE CONNECTIONS

Can I connect ideas in the text to help me understand what the author wants to explain or describe?

ILLUSTRATIONS AND TEXT FEATURES

Does the selection have features, such as an illustration, a map, or a diagram, that can help me to understand the text?

TEXT STRUCTURE

How is the text organized? Can I find a cause or an effect? Are there steps that tell me how to do something? Knowing the text structure helps me understand what I am reading.

 COLLABORATE What do you do when you don't understand something you read?

Look for Text Evidence

When you answer a question about your reading, you often have to look for evidence in the text to support or even find the answer. Here are some tips to help you find what you are looking for.

Maria thinks about her father's words. Pai is right. She and the other children have worked hard for a year. They practiced their dance steps over and over. They even made their own bright colorful costumes.

Stated
Here I can locate information that tells me that Maria put a lot of effort into this celebration.

One week passes. Lots of people line the streets. The children in Maria's group are wearing their sparkling costumes. They know each dance step. They dance to the beat.

Unstated
This text evidence allows me to make the inference that Maria's hard work paid off in the end.

Text Evidence

Sometimes you will find the answers right there in the text. Sometimes you need to look for clues in different parts of text and put the answer in your own words.

It's Stated—Right There!

Some questions ask you to locate details, such as *Who made Maria's costume?* The answers are usually found in a sentence you can point to.

You need to combine clues to answer other questions such as *Why did Maria need to go to practice?* Look in more than one place in the text for the answer.

It's Not Stated—But Here's My Evidence!

Sometimes the answers are not stated in the text. Think of a question like *How did Maria feel when she was marching in the parade?* To answer it, you look for important details or clues. Then you put the clues in your own words to answer the question.

Point to the right there evidence that tells you who made Maria's costume.

Be an Expert Writer

Remember that good writing presents clear ideas. It is well organized and contains evidence and details from reliable sources. See how Alex answered a question about a text he read.

Alex's Model

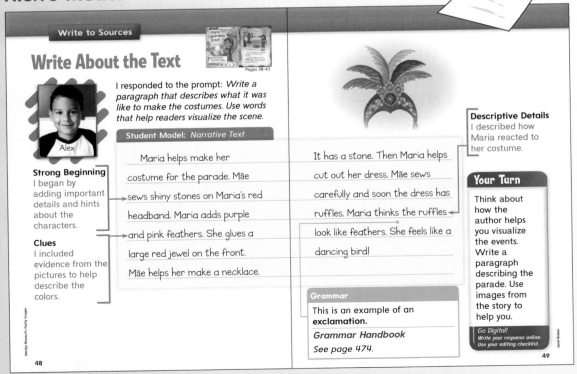

Write to Sources

Write About the Text

Pages 38-43

Alex

I responded to the prompt: *Write a paragraph that describes what it was like to make the costumes. Use words that help readers visualize the scene.*

Student Model: *Narrative Text*

Strong Beginning
I began by adding important details and hints about the characters.

Clues
I included evidence from the pictures to help describe the colors.

Maria helps make her costume for the parade. Mãe sews shiny stones on Maria's red headband. Maria adds purple and pink feathers. She glues a large red jewel on the front. Mãe helps her make a necklace.

It has a stone. Then Maria helps cut out her dress. Mãe sews carefully and soon the dress has ruffles. Maria thinks the ruffles look like feathers. She feels like a dancing bird!

Descriptive Details
I described how Maria reacted to her costume.

Grammar

This is an example of an exclamation.
Grammar Handbook
See page 474.

Your Turn

Think about how the author helps you visualize the events. Write a paragraph describing the parade. Use images from the story to help you.

Go Digital!
Write your response online.
Use your editing checklist.

48

49

W6

Write About the Text

When you write about something you have read closely, introduce your topic clearly. Use details from the text. When you do research, make sure you use reliable sources. Use the checklist below.

Opinions Did I support opinions with facts and evidence? Did I use linking words such as *because* to connect my ideas? Did I write a strong conclusion?

Informative Texts Did I develop the topic with facts from the text? Did I write a conclusion that connected all my information?

Narrative Texts When you write a narrative, you use your imagination to develop real or made-up events. The checklist below will help you write memorable stories.

- **Sequence** Did I use words that help tell the sequence of events?

- **Descriptive Details** Did I include details to describe actions in the narrative?

 COLLABORATE What is your favorite thing to write about? Tell a partner why.

Unit 1 Friends and Family

The Big Idea

How do families and friends learn, grow, and help one another?........**16**

Go Digital! Find all lessons online at www.connected.mcgraw-hill.com.

(t)Marcin Piwowarski; (b)hana/Datacraft/imagenavi/Getty Images

Friends and Family

The Big Idea

How do families and friends learn, grow, and help one another?

Together Is Better

Baseball is no fun at all
  Without a friend to toss the ball.

Camping out would be a bore
  Without your brother to hear you snore.

Piano notes would sound all wrong.
  Without a friend to sing along.

Ice cream would not taste as sweet
  Without your sister to share the treat.

Cleaning up is hard to do
  Without your dad to help out too.

From morning until the day is done
  Friends and family make things fun.

by Constance Keremes

How are families around the world the same and different?

Go Digital!

Families Celebrate

In some parts of the world, families celebrate a holiday called Holi. During Holi, families celebrate Spring.

► Families use colored powder on each other to celebrate flowers blooming.

► Families share a big meal.

Talk About It

Talk with a partner about how your family celebrations are the same and different. Write your ideas on the chart.

Same	Different

Vocabulary

Use the picture and sentence to learn each word.

aside

Juan moves **aside** books on the shelf to find one he likes.

Describe why a person might move aside.

culture

At Chinese New Year, we learn about our **culture**.

Tell about a holiday that shows your culture.

fair

Mom cut the cake so we all got our **fair** share.

What does it mean to be fair?

invited

I **invited** some friends to my birthday party.

Tell about an event you were invited to.

language My friend Naomi speaks and writes in another **language**.

What languages do you know?

plead I had to **plead** with Dad to get a new bike.

What is something you might plead for?

scurries The squirrel **scurries** across the yard.

What is the opposite of scurries?

share I like to **share** music with my sister.

Describe something you share with a family member.

Your Turn

COLLABORATE

Pick three words. Write three questions for your partner to answer.

Go Digital! *Use the online visual glossary*

(t) Christopher Pillitz/Corbis; (tc) Stewart Cohen/Pam Ostrow/Getty Images; (bc) PetStockBoys/Alamy; (b) Mark Edward Atkinson/Getty Images

Maria Celebrates Brazil

? Inquiry Question

What can you learn from a character's actions?

Janet Broxon

22

Maria and her family are in their bright, hot kitchen. "Please, Mãe, por favor!" Maria begs.

Mãe speaks Portuguese. This is the **language** of Brazil. "No matter how much you beg or **plead**, you must go to practice. The parade is next week."

"It's not **fair**," says Maria in English.

Mãe does not know a lot of English. Maria is surprised when she asks, "What is not fair about going to practice? You must do the right thing."

"Ana **invited** me to her house," Maria answers. "I want to go!"

Pai says, "Maria, the parade is important. People from around the world come to see it. They try our food, see how we dress, and how we live. It is a chance for us to **share** our **culture**."

Janet Broxon

24

"I know but I really want to see Ana," says Maria.

Pai says, "Maria, you can see Ana another time. They are giving out costumes at practice today."

Maria thinks about her father's words. Pai is right. She and the other children have worked hard for a year. They practiced their dance steps over and over. They even made their own bright colorful costumes.

"You're right," Maria says to her father. "I'll go to practice. I'll tell Ana I cannot visit her."

One week passes. Lots of people line the streets. The children in Maria's group are wearing their sparkling costumes. They know each dance step. They dance to the beat.

Janet Broxon

The crowd moves **aside** as they make their way down the street.

When the crowd moves away, Maria sees a woman with a camera. She is hurrying. The woman **scurries** by Maria. She puts her camera to her eye. Maria smiles from ear to ear. She is excited to be in the parade. Click! The woman takes a picture of Maria. Maria is proud of her hard work!

Make Connections

How is Maria's family the same and different from other families you know?

Compare Maria's family to your own family. TEXT TO SELF

Visualize

When you visualize, you use the author's words to form pictures in your mind about a story.

 Find Text Evidence

On page 25 of "Maria Celebrates Brazil," what words does the author use to help you visualize the costumes?

page 25

Maria thinks about her father's words. Pai is right. She and the other children have worked hard for a year. They practiced their dance steps over and over. They even made their own bright colorful costumes.

I read that the children made bright and colorful costumes. This helps me visualize the parade.

Your Turn

COLLABORATE

What does Maria do in the parade? Reread page 26 and visualize parts of the story that help you answer the question.

Character, Setting, Events

A character is a person or animal in a story. The setting of a story tells when and where a story takes place. The events are what happens.

 Find Text Evidence

As I read page 23 of "Maria Celebrates Brazil," I learn who the characters are, what they do, and where the story takes place.

Character	Setting	Events
Maria, Mãe Pai	Maria's kitchen	Maria wants to miss practice to go to her friend's house.

Your Turn COLLABORATE

Continue reading the story. Then fill in the information in the graphic organizer.

Go Digital!
Use the interactive graphic organizer

Realistic Fiction

The story "*Maria Celebrates Brazil*," is realistic fiction. **Realistic fiction**:

- is a made-up story with characters that could be real people.
- has a beginning, middle, and end.

Find Text Evidence

I can tell that "Maria Celebrates Brazil" is realistic fiction. The characters are like real people. Also, the story has a beginning, middle and end.

page 24

"It's not **fair**," says Maria in English.

Māe does not know a lot of English. Maria is surprised when she asks, "What is not fair about going to practice? You must do the right thing."

"Ana **invited** me to her house," Maria answers. "I want to go!"

Pai says, "Maria, the parade is important. People from around the world come to see it. They try our food, see how we dress, and how we live. It is a chance for us to **share** our **culture**."

24

Story Structure

In the beginning of the story, I read that Maria wants to skip practice and go to a friend's house.

Your Turn

COLLABORATE

Tell about events that happen in the middle and end of the story.

Root Words

To understand the meaning of a word you do not know, try to separate the root word from the endings such as *–ed*, or *-ing*.

 Find Text Evidence

As I read the word hurrying, *I can split the root word* hurry *from the ending* -ing, *which can mean something happening right now. I think* hurrying *means "moving quickly right now."*

Maria sees a woman with a camera. She is hurrying.

Your Turn

Use root words to figure out the meanings of other words in *"Maria Celebrates Brazil."*
    worked, *page 25*
    practiced, *page 25*

Janet Broxon

Write About the Text

Pages 22–27

Alex

I responded to the prompt: *Write a paragraph that describes what it was like to make the costumes. Use words that help readers visualize the scene.*

Strong Beginning
I began by adding important details and hints about the characters.

Clues
I included evidence from the pictures to help describe the colors.

Student Model: *Narrative Text*

Maria helps make her costume for the parade. Mãe sews shiny stones on Maria's red headband. Maria adds purple and pink feathers. She glues a large red jewel on the front. Mãe helps her make a necklace.

It has a stone. Then Maria helps cut out her dress. Mãe sews carefully and soon the dress has ruffles. Maria thinks the ruffles look like feathers. She feels like a dancing bird!

Descriptive Details

I described how Maria reacted to her costume.

Your Turn

Think about how the author helps you visualize the events. Write a paragraph describing the parade. Use images from the story to help you.

Go Digital!
Write your response online.
Use your editing checklist.

Grammar

This is an example of an **exclamation**.

Grammar Handbook
See page 474.

Janet Broxon

Our Pet Friends

Pets can be our friends. Pets come in all shapes and sizes.

▶ Pets can make us laugh.

▶ Pets can help us.

▶ Pets love us.

Talk About It

Talk with a partner about having pets as friends. Write words on the word web that tell how pets are our friends.

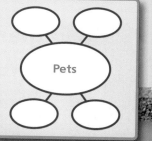

Pets

Vocabulary

Use the picture and sentence to learn each word.

decide I **decide** to have juice and cereal for breakfast.

What did you decide to eat for breakfast today?

different The brown kitten is **different** than the orange kitten.

How are a horse and a cat different?

friendship Because of their **friendship**, the kids played together a lot.

Tell about your friendship with a friend.

glance I **glance** to see what book my sister is reading.

What word is the opposite of glance?

proper It is **proper** to wipe your mouth during a meal.

Tell how to act in a proper way at the library.

relationship Our teacher has a good **relationship** with our class.

What relationship do you have with your best friend?

stares Helen **stares** at her friend.

What do you look like when you stare at something?

trade Don and Luis **trade** baseball cards.

What things do you trade with your friend?

Your Turn

COLLABORATE

Pick three words. Write three questions for your partner to answer.

Go Digital! *Use the online visual glossary*

Finding Cal

? Inquiry Question

What can you learn from a character's actions?

Marcin Piwowarski

Dear Diary,

It took Dad a long time to **decide**. He finally made up his mind. Dad came to my room tonight. He said I could get a dog! But it has to be a small or medium-sized dog. We will go to the animal shelter tomorrow.

Medium Dog

Small Dog

Dear Diary,

Wow! There are so many **different** dogs at the shelter. There are big and little dogs. Some have soft fur and some have wiry hair.

Dad and I walked to one dog's cage. The tag said the dog's name was Cal. One quick **glance** at the cute dog, and I knew he was for me. Dad said, "Look, Jake! Look at how Cal **stares** at you." It was true! His eyes were wide open. He was looking right at me.

Jack   Spot   Sam   Cal

Marcin Piwowarski

We put Cal on a leash and took him to a fenced yard. Cal smiled and stared at me. Cal wanted to play. In minutes he learned the **proper**, or correct, way to sit. He could walk on a leash nicely, too. I patted him on the head, and he licked my hand.

Cal licking my hand!

Dad said, "I see a real connection between you and Cal." I agreed. We already had a good **relationship**.

Soon we were on our way home. Cal was nervous so I tried to make him feel better. I scratched his ears, and he liked it.

Dear Diary,

It has been a while since I have written. Cal has learned many new tricks like how to roll over. I have learned from Cal, too.

Cal's Tricks!

Cal walks with Dad and me to school every day. Each night, Dad reads me a story. Cal lies next to me. I would not **trade** him for any other dog. I will keep him because our **friendship** is very special. Finding Cal was worth the wait!

Make Connections

How is Cal an important friend to Jake?

Compare Jake's pet Cal to your pet or a pet you know. Tell how each pet is a good friend. TEXT TO SELF

Ask and Answer Questions

When you read, you can ask questions to help you think about parts of the story that you may have missed or do not understand.

 Find Text Evidence

After reading page 40 of "Finding Cal," I ask myself, "What helped Jake decide to take Cal home?"

page 41

to a fenced yard. Cal smiled and stared at me. Cal wanted to play. In minutes he learned the **proper**, or correct, way to sit. He could walk on a leash nicely, too. I patted him on the head, and he licked my hand.

Cal licking my hand!

I read that Cal smiled and stared at Jake. Cal wants to play with Jake. From this, I understand that Cal is already special to Jake.

Your Turn

COLLABORATE

Think of a question you have about the story. Reread the parts of the story that help you answer the question.

Character, Setting, Events

The pictures and text give you details about the characters, setting, and events in a story.

 Find Text Evidence

As I look at the pictures and read the text on page 39 of "Finding Cal," I see details about the character, setting, and events.

Character	Setting	Events
Jake	Jake's Home	Jake is excited to be getting a dog.

Your Turn

Continue reading the story. Then fill in the information in the graphic organizer.

Go Digital!
Use the interactive graphic organizer

Fiction

The story "Finding Cal" is Fiction. Fiction:
- has made up characters and events.
- has a beginning, middle, and end.

Find Text Evidence

I can use what I read to tell that "Finding Cal" is fiction. The story has a beginning, middle, and end.

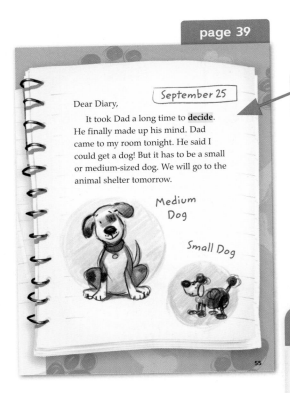

page 39

September 25

Dear Diary,

It took Dad a long time to **decide**. He finally made up his mind. Dad came to my room tonight. He said I could get a dog! But it has to be a small or medium-sized dog. We will go to the animal shelter tomorrow.

Medium Dog

Small Dog

55

Story Structure

In the beginning of the story, I read that a family decides to adopt a dog.

COLLABORATE

Your Turn

Tell about events that happen in the middle and end of the story.

Context Clues

To understand the meaning of a word you do not know, look at the other words in the sentence for clues.

 Find Text Evidence

I'm not sure what the word "nervous" means. The words "make him feel better" make me think Cal was not relaxed. I think "nervous" means not relaxed.

> Cal was nervous so
> I tried to make him
> feel better.

Your Turn

COLLABORATE

Use context clues to figure out the meanings of other words in "Finding Cal."
connection, *page 42*
leash, *page 41*

Write About the Text

Pages 38–43

James

I responded to the prompt: *Write a diary entry to add to the end of the story. Show Cal and Jake's relationship.*

Student Model: *Narrative Text*

October 15

Dear Diary,

I think that Cal misses me when I go to school. He jumps up when Dad and I come in.

He tries to lick my face.

Cal dashes to the door when I come. He rolls over and begs.

Organization
I wrote *Dear Diary* and put a date, just like Jake did in "Finding Cal."

Word Choice
I tried to paint a picture of Cal by using precise words.

Steve Prezant/Image Source/Getty Images

Grammar

The **subject** of this sentence is *Cal and I*. The subject tells who plays outside.

Grammar Handbook

See page 475.

After we have a snack, Cal and I play outside. I am teaching him more tricks.

I miss Cal during school. I think he needs me. I will not let him down.

Descriptive Details
I included details to show Jake's thoughts and feelings.

Your Turn

Add a diary entry to the beginning of the story. Write about Jake's conversation with his dad about dogs.

Go Digital!
Write your response online.
Use your editing checklist.

Marcin Piwowarski

How do we care for animals?

Go Digital!

Caring for Animals

All animals have needs. People give the animals what they need to live.

Animals need:

▶ fresh food and water each day

▶ air to breathe

▶ a safe place to live

Talk About It

Work with a partner. Tell how people care for animals. Write your ideas on the word web.

Animal Care

Vocabulary

Use the picture and sentence to learn each word.

allowed — Dogs are not **allowed** on the beach.

What things are allowed at school?

care — I help **care** for my little brother.

Tell how you take care of your belongings.

excited — The girls were **excited** to play with their new puppy.

What would you be excited about seeing or doing?

needs — Food and water are some of the **needs** of every animal.

What are your needs?

(t) Tom Hoenig/Getty Images; (tc) Somos Images/Alamy; (bc) Nancy Ney/Getty Images; (b) Steve Lyne/Getty Images

roam Lions **roam** the plains in Africa.

Describe how you move when you roam.

safe Wearing a seatbelt keeps me **safe** in the car.

How can you stay safe when riding a bike?

wandered A bear cub **wandered** away from its mother.

What is the opposite of wandered?

wild Bears and raccoons live in the **wild**.

Name some animals you have seen in the wild.

COLLABORATE

Your Turn

Pick three words. Write three questions for your partner to answer.

Go Digital! *Use the online visual glossary*

Taking Care of Pepper

Inquiry Question

What can our families and pets teach us?

Have you ever been on a farm? Jack lives on a farm. He has a horse named Pepper. Jack helps take **care** of Pepper. Looking after a horse is a big job. A horse has many **needs**. There are a lot of things a horse must have to live.

Pepper stomps his hoof and nods his head when he sees Jack.

Every morning, Jack wakes up at 5:00 a.m. He and his father go to Pepper's stall. The stall keeps Pepper **safe** from bad weather and other dangers.

When Pepper sees Jack, the horse gets **excited**. Jack smiles when the horse gets all worked up.

First, Jack gives Pepper hay to eat. While Pepper eats, Jack cleans Pepper's stall. He shovels out the dirty hay and sawdust. Then he puts down fresh padding.

Tom Joslyn/Alamy

Next, Jack strokes Pepper's brown coat and it feels smooth. Then Jack leaves to go to school. But his work is not done!

At 3:00 p.m., Jack rides the bus back home. He has a snack and does his homework. Next, his mother gives him an apple for Pepper. Then they go to visit Pepper.

Jack feeds Pepper hay and fresh water every day.

Andy Crawford and Kit Houghton/Dorling Kindersley/Getty Images

Jack and his mom find Pepper in a field. Pepper is **allowed** to **roam**. He can walk all around the field. He was drinking after having **wandered** the field. All that walking here and there made Pepper thirsty!

Now it is time for Pepper's exercise. In the **wild**, horses run many hours a day. But Pepper does not live out in nature. Jack must make sure Pepper gets the exercise he needs.

Pepper must have exercise each day.

Jack puts the saddle on Pepper. He places the bit in Pepper's mouth. Mom does the same thing with her horse, and they ride horses together.

When they are finished riding, Jack grooms Pepper. He brushes his mane, tail, and fur.

Finally, Jack gives Pepper more hay and refills his water bucket. "See you in the morning," Jack says. Pepper nods his head as if to say, "Yes, I'll be waiting!"

Jack's Dad checks for rocks in Pepper's hooves. If he sees one, he must get it out.

Make Connections

How do people care for horses?

Compare the needs of a horse and another pet you know. Which needs more care? TEXT TO SELF

Ask and Answer Questions

When you read, asking questions helps you think about parts of the story you may have missed or do not understand.

 Find Text Evidence

On page 55 of "Taking Care of Pepper," I read that a horse has many needs. I ask myself, "What things does a horse need?"

> **page 56**
>
> Every morning, Jack wakes up at 5:00 a.m. He and his father go to Pepper's stall. The stall keeps Pepper **safe** from bad weather and other dangers.
>
> When Pepper sees Jack, the horse gets **excited**. Jack smiles when the horse gets all worked up.
>
> First, Jack gives Pepper hay to eat. While Pepper eats, Jack cleans Pepper's stall. He shovels out the dirty hay and sawdust. Then he puts down fresh padding.
>
> 56

I read that Jack feeds Pepper hay. I understand that Jack takes care of Pepper and gives him what he needs.

COLLABORATE

Your Turn

Think of a question to ask about Pepper's needs. Reread parts of the selection to find the answer to the question.

Key Details

You can find important details in the photos and text of a selection.

 Find Text Evidence

As I read the text and photo caption on page 56 of "Taking Care of Pepper," I understand that Jack cares for Pepper. Pepper recognizes Jack and shows that he cares for him, too.

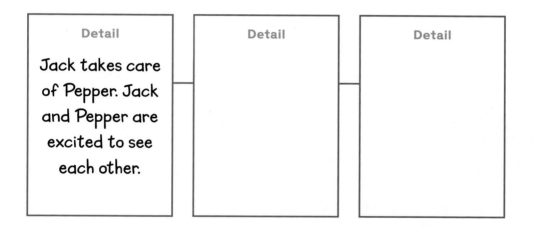

Detail	Detail	Detail
Jack takes care of Pepper. Jack and Pepper are excited to see each other.		

COLLABORATE

Your Turn

Continue reading the selection. Then fill in the information in the graphic organizer.

Go Digital!
Use the interactive graphic organizer

Narrative Nonfiction

The selection "Taking Care of Pepper" is Narrative Nonfiction. **Narrative Nonfiction**:

- is about real people, things, or events.
- is told by a narrator.
- can have photos and captions.

🔍 Find Text Evidence

I know that "Taking Care of Pepper" is a narrative nonfiction because it tells how a boy cares for a real horse. The photos and captions tell more about how to care for a horse.

page 56

Pepper stomps his hoof and nods his head when he sees Jack.

Every morning, Jack wakes up at 5:00 a.m. He and his father go to Pepper's stall. The stall keeps Pepper **safe** from bad weather and other dangers.

When Pepper sees Jack, the horse gets **excited**. Jack smiles when the horse gets all worked up.

First, Jack gives Pepper hay to eat. While Pepper eats, Jack cleans Pepper's stall. He shovels out the dirty hay and sawdust. Then he puts down fresh padding.

56

Text Features

- **Photos** are pictures.
- **Captions** are words that tell about a photo.

COLLABORATE

Your Turn

Find other photos with captions. Tell what you learn from them.

Root Words

To understand the meaning of a word you do not know, try to break up the word into word parts. You can split the root word from the ending such as *–ed*, *-es*, or *-ing*.

 Find Text Evidence

As I read the word finished, *I can break out the root word* finish, *which means "to come to an end," from the ending -ed, which can mean "happened in the past." I think the word* finished *means "came to an end."*

> When they are finished riding, Jack grooms Pepper.

Your Turn   COLLABORATE

Use root words to figure out the meanings of other words in "Taking Care of Pepper."

brushes, *page 59*
waiting, *page 59*

Pages 54–59

Write About the Text

Sophie

I answered the question: *In your opinion, is taking care of a horse easy or hard? Explain why using examples from the text.*

Student Model: *Opinion*

I think taking care of a horse is hard. The text tells me that Jack feeds Pepper hay at 5 in the morning. Then Jack has to clean out the stall with a shovel. Next he feeds Pepper and gives the horse water. That all happens before school begins!

Strong Beginning
I introduced the topic, answered the question, and stated my opinion.

Sequence
I organized my ideas. I used the order that Jack cares for Pepper each day based on the text.

(l)©Jose Luis Pelaez Inc/Blend Images LLC; r)©iStockphoto.com/nancykennedy

Jack rides Pepper every afternoon. I think that part would be fun and easy, but after riding, Jack has to brush and feed Pepper. I think people who care for horses are busy!

Grammar

The **predicate** in this sentence tells what Jack does.

Grammar Handbook

See page 475.

Word Choice

I used a linking word to show my opinion on caring for a horse.

Your Turn

In your opinion, would you be good at taking care of a horse? Tell why or why not using details from the text.

Go Digital!
Write your response online.
Use your editing checklist.

What happens when families work together?

Go Digital!

How Families Work

This family is working together to make a pie. Working together gets chores done and can be fun! There are many ways families work together.

► Families do jobs at home, such as cooking and cleaning.

► Families shop together for food and clothing. They think about the cost of the items.

Talk About It

Talk with a partner about how your family works together. List your ideas on the web.

Families Work Together

Vocabulary

Use the picture and sentence to learn each word.

check Mom will **check** to make sure Tina's helmet fits.

When would you need to check something?

choose Julian will **choose** a shirt to wear.

Tell about a time when you had to choose something.

chores Sierra must finish her **chores** before she can play.

What is another word for chores?

cost Jordan asked, "How much does the shirt **cost**?"

What are two things that cost a lot of money?

customers

The **customers** lined up to buy lemonade.

Why would a store like to have a lot of customers?

jobs

Nurse and doctor are two **jobs** at a hospital.

Name some other jobs people have.

spend

William decided to **spend** his money on a snack.

Name two things parents spend their money on.

tools

Tom and his dad used **tools** to build a birdhouse.

What are some tools you have seen people use?

COLLABORATE

Your Turn

Pick three words. Write three questions for your partner to answer.

Go Digital! *Use the online visual glossary*

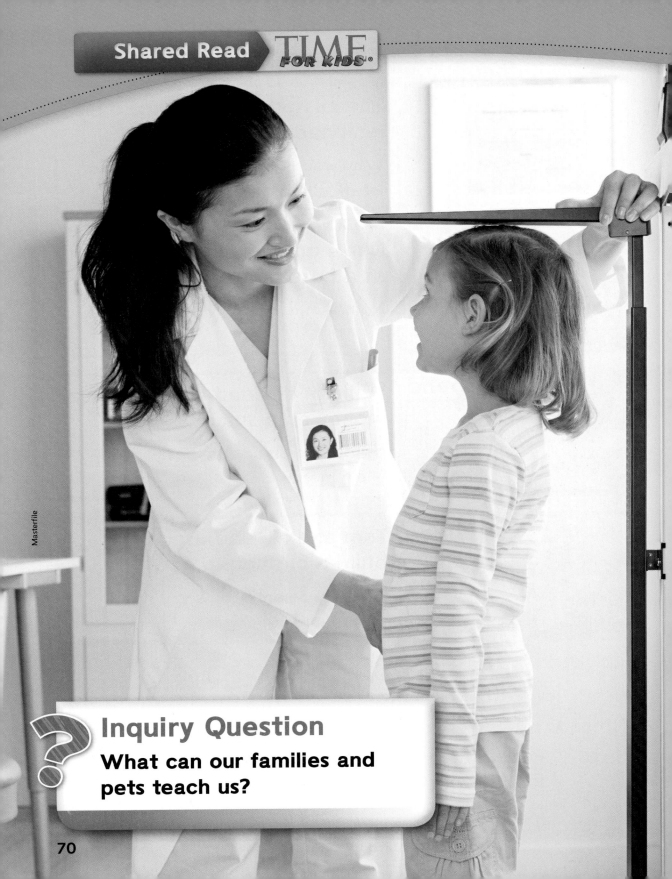

Masterfile

? Inquiry Question

What can our families and pets teach us?

Families Work!

Ellen Yung had a busy day at work! She put a cast on a broken arm, used a bandage to cover a deep cut, and helped twenty patients. Ellen is a doctor for children. **Customers** can get sick at any time, so pediatricians work long hours. They have hard **jobs**.

Ellen's husband works long hours, too. Steve is a firefighter. At the fire house, he makes sure the **tools** work properly. He **checks** the hoses and fire trucks. At the fire, Steve rescues people from hot flames and smoke. The firefighters all work together to put out the fire.

PBNJ Productions/Blend Images/Getty Images

When a fire alarm sounds, Steve suits up quickly.

71

At home, the Yung family works together too. Hanna sets the table for dinner. She also helps wash the dishes. Everyone has weekly **chores**. Mom and Hanna do the dusting and mopping. Dad and her brother, Zac, do the laundry. They wash, dry, and fold the clothes. Mom makes a shopping list each week. She lists items they need and things they want.

A short time ago, Zac wanted a new laptop. The family needed a new washing machine. They could only **spend** money on one item. Both **cost** the same. They had to **choose**. Clean clothes are needed for school and work. A new laptop is nice, but did Zac need it? Ellen and Steve thought about their family's needs. They decided to buy the washing machine.

Hanna's brother, Zac, helps with the meals.

What Are Some Needs and Wants?

Needs	Wants
Water	Skateboard
Food	Video game
Shelter	Basketball
Clothing	

Zac knows that his parents have busy jobs. They bring home money to pay for their needs and wants. They needed that washing machine. Zac still wants a laptop. The family has decided to save some money each week so they can buy it in the future.

Make Connections

How does the Yung family work together?

How is your family similar or different from the family in the story? TEXT TO SELF

Ask and Answer Questions

When you read, asking questions helps you think about parts of the story you may have missed or do not understand.

Find Text Evidence

As I read page 72 of "Families Work!" I ask myself, "Why did the family buy a washing machine instead of a laptop?" I will reread to find the answer to my question.

page 72

A short time ago, Zac wanted a new laptop. The family needed a new washing machine. They could only **spend** money on one item. Both **cost** the same. They had to **choose**. Clean clothes are needed for school and work. A new laptop is nice, but did Zac need it? Ellen and Steve thought about their family's needs. They decided to buy the washing machine.

Hanna's brother, Zac, helps with the meals.

I read that Zac wanted a laptop, but the family needed a washing machine. I understand the family had to make a choice.

Your Turn

COLLABORATE

Think of a question you have about the story. Reread the parts of the selection to find the answer to the question.

Key Details

Key details are important pieces of information in a text. Key details are found in the text and photos of a selection.

 Find Text Evidence

As I read and look at the photos on pages 70 and 71 of "Families Work!" I understand that Ellen Yung is a pediatrician. Her husband, Steve, is a firefighter. They both work away from home.

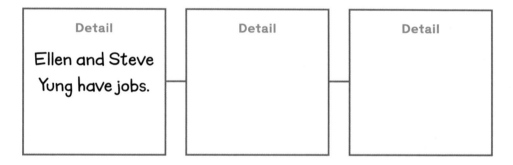

Detail	Detail	Detail
Ellen and Steve Yung have jobs.		

Your Turn COLLABORATE

Continue reading the selection. Then fill in the key details in the graphic organizer.

Go Digital!
Use the interactive graphic organizer

Expository Text

"Families Work!" is an expository text.

Expository text:

- gives facts and information about a topic.
- can have text features.

🔍 **Find Text Evidence**

I know "Families Work!" is expository text because it gives facts about how family members work to meet their needs. It also has text features.

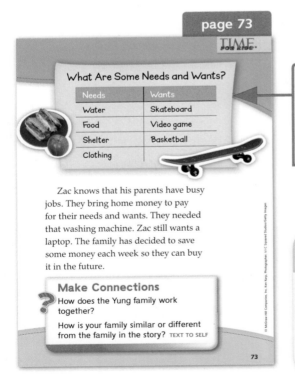

page 73

TIME FOR KIDS

What Are Some Needs and Wants?

Needs	Wants
Water	Skateboard
Food	Video game
Shelter	Basketball
Clothing	

Zac knows that his parents have busy jobs. They bring home money to pay for their needs and wants. They needed that washing machine. Zac still wants a laptop. The family has decided to save some money each week so they can buy it in the future.

❓ Make Connections

How does the Yung family work together?

How is your family similar or different from the family in the story? TEXT TO SELF

73

Text Features

- A **chart** shows information in an organized way. Facts may be in rows and columns.

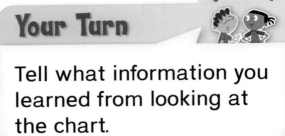

Your Turn COLLABORATE

Tell what information you learned from looking at the chart.

Inflectional Endings

To understand the meaning of a word you do not know, separate the root word from its ending, such as *-s, -es,* or *-ed.*

 Find Text Evidence

I see the word dishes. *I can separate the root word* dish, *which means "a plate or bowl used for holding food," from the inflectional ending* -es, *which can mean "more than one." I think the word* dishes *means "more than one dish."*

She also helps wash the dishes.

COLLABORATE

Your Turn

Name the inflectional ending and the meaning of these words in "Families Work!":
hours, *page 71*
helped, *page 71*

Write About the Text

Pages 70-73

I answered the question: *What was the author's purpose for including a Needs and Wants chart in the selection?*

Lee

Student Model: *Informative Text*

The author includes a Needs and Wants chart to help me understand how families spend and save money. The chart tells me things that every family needs to live, such as food, water, shelter, and clothing.

Sentence Fluency
I wrote short and long sentences to make my writing interesting.

Supporting Details
I added information from the chart to support my answer.

Needs	Wants
Water	Skateboard
Food	Video game
Shelter	Basketball
Clothing	

Grammar

This is an example of expanding a **sentence** by **combining** ideas.

Grammar Handbook

See page 476.

Families pay for these things first. Parents and kids save the money that is left over. In the future, they might use the money they save to buy the things they want, like washing machines, laptops, or video games.

Strong Conclusion
The last sentence I wrote sums up my answer.

Your Turn

How do families make choices about how to spend their money? Use evidence from the text to support your answer.

Go Digital!
Write your response online.
Use your editing checklist.

How do friends depend on each other?

Go Digital!

fStop Images - Lisa Sciascia/Brand X Pictures/Getty Images

Friends
Help Each Other

These friends are helping each other find out where they are on the map. Their actions help each other. There are many ways we depend on our friends.

▶ We depend on our friends to teach us things.

▶ We need our friends to give us comfort when we are hurt or upset.

Talk About It

Talk with a partner about how friends depend on each other. Then write your ideas on the web.

Friends Depend on Each Other

Vocabulary

Use the picture and sentence to learn each word.

actions The girl's **actions** helped her team win the soccer game.

What actions might help you do well in school?

afraid Our dog is **afraid** of thunder.

What things are you afraid of?

depend Nick **depends** on his dad to help him learn to ride a bike.

What do you depend on your parents for?

nervously Maya waited **nervously** for her swim race to begin.

How would you look if you were acting nervously?

peered

The cat **peered** through the hole in the barn.

What would you see if you peered through a window at home?

perfectly

The orange is **perfectly** round.

Name something in your house that is perfectly square.

rescue

We watched the boy **rescue** the cat from the tree.

What is another word for rescue?

secret

Mandy whispered a **secret** to me.

What is special about a secret?

Your Turn

COLLABORATE

Pick three words. Write three questions for your partner to answer.

Go Digital! *Use the online visual glossary*

Little Flap Learns to Fly

? Inquiry Question

How do characters make decisions?

Little Flap was happy living in his nest. His friends, Fluff and Tuff, lived in the nest next to him. Every morning they sang songs together. Their parents brought them worms to eat.

One day Fluff asked, "Can we get our own worms?"

Tuff said, "We can if we learn to fly."

Fluff said, "Yes! Let's learn to fly."

Little Flap **peered** over the edge of
his nest. It was very high up. When he
looked down, the ground seemed very far
away. He felt scared! He was too **afraid** to
tell his friends about his fear so he kept his
feelings a **secret**.

Fluff said, "Let's practice flapping our
wings. It will make them strong. Watch."

Tuff and Little Flap watched Fluff.
Then they copied her **actions**.

Soon it was time to fly. Little Flap could no longer keep his feelings a secret. He asked, "Will I fall? I don't want to get hurt."

Tuff said, "You can **depend** on Fluff and me. We're your friends."

Fluff said, "I have an idea. We will go first and show you how. Then you can try. If you fall, Tuff and I will **rescue** you."

Tuff said, "Yes, we can save you!" Tuff and Fluff jumped out of the nest. They flew!

Little Flap looked down **nervously**. He still felt uneasy, but he felt braver with his friends. "Okay," he said. "Let's try!"

The three birds stood together on the branch. They counted, "One! Two! Three!" Then they flapped their wings fast and jumped. Little Flap lifted into the air.

"You're flying just right!" said Fluff.

"You're flying **perfectly**!" said Tuff.

All three little birds landed
in a patch of soft, green grass.

Little Flap said, "Now I know I can
always depend on you, Fluff and Tuff!
You are my friends."

Then he found a big, juicy worm
and shared it with his friends.

Now Little Flap likes flying!

Make Connections

Describe how Little Flap depends on his friends.

Discuss a time when you depended on your friends. TEXT TO SELF

Visualize

When you visualize, you form pictures in your mind about the characters, setting, and events in the story.

Find Text Evidence

After reading page 85 of "Little Flap Learns to Fly," I know that Little Flap is thinking about flying. On page 86 what words does the author use to help readers visualize the nest?

page 86

Little Flap **peered** over the edge of his nest. It was very high up. When he looked down, the ground seemed very far

I read that the nest was very high up and the ground seemed far away. From this, I can visualize the nest.

COLLABORATE

Your Turn

Reread page 89. What words help you visualize where the birds landed?

Key Details

You can learn important information in a story by looking for key details in the illustrations.

 Find Text Evidence

As I read page 86 of "Little Flap Learns to Fly," I can look at the illustrations to find key details about the characters and events.

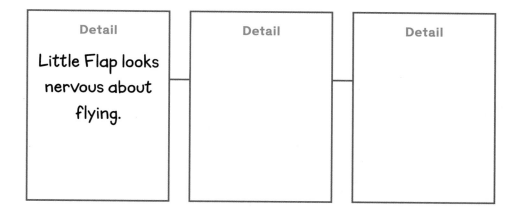

Detail	Detail	Detail
Little Flap looks nervous about flying.		

Your Turn

Continue reading the story. Does Little Flap learn to fly? List the key details in your graphic organizer.

Go Digital!
Use the interactive graphic organizer

Fantasy

"Little Flap Learns to Fly" is a fantasy story.
A **Fantasy**:

- is a made-up story.
- has imaginary characters that could not be real.

🔍 Find Text Evidence

I can use what I read to tell that "Little Flap Learns to Fly" is a fantasy story. The story has made-up characters.

page 84

Shared Read > Genre · Fantasy

Little Flap Learns to Fly

? Inquiry Question
How do characters make decisions?

84

Use Illustrations

I see the birds have clothing on. I know birds in real life do not wear clothing. This must be fantasy.

Your Turn COLLABORATE

Find two other things in the story that could not happen in real life. Tell why this story is a fantasy.

Inflectional Endings

To understand the meaning of a word you do not know, you can separate the root word from the ending, such as *-ed* or *-s.*

 Find Text Evidence

I'm not sure what the word looked *means. I know the root word* look *means "to see." The ending* -ed *means this action happened in the past. The word* looked *means "saw something in the past."*

When he looked down, the ground seemed very far away.

Your Turn

Use the endings to figure out the meanings of these words in "Little Flap Learns to Fly."
friends, *page 86*
counted, *page 88*

Tim Beaumont

Write About the Text

Pages 84–89

I responded to the prompt: *Add an event to the story where Flap shares his worm with his friends. Tell why he shared it.*

Anita

Ideas
I thought about the event of Little Flap catching the worm.

Supporting Details
I added information from "Little Flap Learns to Fly" to illustrate my writing.

Student Model: *Narrative Text*

Little Flap wanted to do something nice for his friends. What could he do? Flap thought of that big, juicy worm. Little Flap was good at catching worms. He ran until he caught it. It wiggled in his mouth.

Descriptive Details
I used actions to help describe Little Flap catching the worm.

Fluff and Tuff were very excited. Little Flap shared the worm because his friends loved worms. The friends talked and laughed together. It had been a very big day.

Grammar

This is an example of a **complete sentence.**

Grammar Handbook See page 474.

Your Turn

Add an event to the story. Have Fluff tell how he convinced Flap to fly. Include details in your writing.

Go Digital!
Write your response online.
Use your editing checklist.

Tim Beaumont

Contents

Sentences

Sentences

A **sentence** tells a complete thought.

Tom feeds the cat.

Your Turn Write each group of words. Write "complete" next to the complete sentence.

1. The dog runs outside.
2. Digs in the yard.

Kinds of Sentences

Every sentence begins with a **capital letter** and ends with an **end mark**.

A **statement** tells something. It ends with a period.	*Tara can read music.*
A **question** asks something. It ends with a question mark.	*Do you like this song?*
A **command** tells someone to do something. It ends with a period.	*Sing along with me.*
An **exclamation** shows strong feeling. It ends with an exclamation mark.	*We sound great together!*

Your Turn Write each sentence. Then tell what kind of sentence it is.

1. Anna plays in a band.
2. Does she sing?
3. We love the new song!
4. Listen to the drums.

Subjects in Sentences

The **subject** in a sentence tells who or what does something.

Our teacher reads the story.

Your Turn **Write each sentence. Underline the subject.**

1. Ann listens to the news.
2. Mom looks outside.
3. Strong winds begin to blow.
4. Ann and Mom make plans.
5. The family prepares for the storm.

Predicates in Sentences

The **predicate** in a sentence tells what the subject does or is.

Our teacher reads the story.

Your Turn **Write each sentence. Underline each predicate.**

1. Rosa listens to the news.
2. She hears about the storm.
3. Her two brothers close the windows.
4. Everyone is excited.
5. The heavy rain falls at night.

Sentences

Combining Sentences: Subjects

When two sentences have the same predicate, you can use the word **and** to combine the subjects.

Trina <u>went to the movies</u>. Kim <u>went to the movies</u>. Trina <u>and</u> Kim went to the movies.

Your Turn Use **and** to combine each pair of sentences. Write the new sentence.

1. Shawn sat down. Kent sat down.
2. Brianna wanted pizza. Kent wanted pizza.
3. The pizza smelled good. The pasta smelled good.
4. Kent asked for water. I asked for water.
5. Brianna thanked the waiter. Shawn thanked the waiter.

Nouns

A **noun** is a word that names a person, place, or thing.

My brother left his book at the library.

    ↑   ↑   ↑

  person   *thing*   *place*

Your Turn Write each sentence. Draw a line under each noun.

1. My family lives in a small town.
2. Our father works in the city.
3. The cousins share stories.

Common and Proper Nouns

Common nouns name general people, places, or things.

The <u>woman</u> drives her <u>car</u> down the <u>street</u>.

Proper nouns name specific people, places, or things.

<u>Jenny</u> walks <u>Whiskers</u> down <u>Park Street</u>.

Your Turn Write each sentence. Underline each common noun. Circle each proper noun.

1. My cousins are going to Mexico.
2. Their plane leaves from Chicago.
3. Lori will bring a camera.
4. My family will stay on Pine Street.

Nouns

Days, Months, and Holidays

Some proper nouns name **days of the week, months,** and **holidays.** They begin with capital letters.

> *Our homework is due on <u>Monday</u>. (day of the week)*
> *My birthday is in <u>April</u>. (month of the year)*
> *We will travel for <u>Thanksgiving</u>. (holiday)*

Your Turn Write each sentence correctly. Begin each proper noun with a capital letter.

1. School is closed next monday.
2. It will be memorial day.
3. This was the warmest may ever.

Singular and Plural Nouns

A noun that names only one thing is **singular**.

A noun that names more than one thing is **plural**.

Add -*s* to form the plural of most nouns.

> *The large river split into two <u>rivers</u>.*

Add -*es* to form the plural of nouns that end in *s, sh, ch,* or *x. This box is bigger than the other <u>boxes</u>.*

Your Turn Write each sentence. Make the noun in ( ) name more than one.

1. I have two (wish).
2. First, I need new (sock).
3. Next, I want three (book).

More Plural Nouns

If a word ends in a consonant plus *y*, change the *y* to *i* and add -*es* to form the plural.

> *My mother's <u>berry</u> pie has three kinds of <u>berries</u>.*

Some nouns change their spelling to name more than one. Others don't change at all.

Singular	Plural
man	men
woman	women
child	children
tooth	teeth
mouse	mice
foot	feet
fish	fish
sheep	sheep

Your Turn **Write each sentence. Make the noun in ( ) name more than one.**

1. The (child) went to a farm.
2. How many (sheep) did they see?
3. The barn was thirty (foot) high!
4. Four (pony) played in a field.
5. Workers picked (cherry) from the trees.

Nouns

Collective Nouns

A **collective noun** names a group that acts together as a singular thing.

The <u>team</u> runs out onto the field.

Your Turn Write each sentence. Underline each collective noun.

1. My family plays music.
2. I may start a band.
3. The group needs to practice.

Singular and Plural Possessive Nouns

A **possessive noun** is a noun that shows who or what owns something. Add an **apostrophe (')** and an -*s* to a singular noun to make it possessive.

The dog grabbed our <u>father's</u> hat.

Add just an apostrophe to most plural nouns to make them possessive. *The two <u>brothers'</u> bikes are both red.*

Add an apostrophe and an -*s* to form the possessive of plural nouns that do not end in -*s*.

The men went to get the <u>women's</u> coats.

Your Turn Write each sentence. Use the possessive form of the noun in ( ) .

1. I study at my (friend) house.
2. What are his (parents) names?
3. Listen to the (children) songs!

Action Verbs

An **action verb** is a word that shows action.

The runners <u>race</u> to the finish line.

Your Turn Write each sentence. Draw a line under each action verb.

1. We drive to the beach.
2. My father swims in the ocean.
3. My sisters build a sand castle.
4. My brother collects shells and rocks.
5. Mom dives into the water and splashes us.

Linking Verbs

A **linking verb** connects the subject to the rest of the sentence. It does not show action. Linking verbs include: *be, am, is, are, was, were, will be.*

Our teacher <u>is</u> a wonderful actor.

Your Turn Write each sentence. Draw a line under each linking verb.

1. The class play is a comedy.
2. The lines are hard to learn.
3. My best friends were clowns.
4. I am excited about my role.
5. The setting will be a circus.

Verbs

Present-Tense Verbs

Present-tense verbs tell what is happening now.
Add *-s* or *-es* to tell what one person or thing is doing.

> *The man <u>looks</u> at the sky. He <u>watches</u> the dark clouds.*

Your Turn Write each sentence in the present tense. Use the correct form of the verb in ( ).

1. The rain (start) to fall.
2. The horse (run) into the barn.
3. Water (rush) down the hill.

Past-Tense Verbs

Past-tense verbs tell about actions in the past. Most past-tense verbs end with *-ed*.

> *The players <u>kicked</u> the ball into the woods.*

For verbs like *drop,* double the final consonant before adding *-ed.*
For verbs like *race,* drop the e before adding *-ed.*

> *The principal <u>tapped</u> the glass and <u>raised</u> the window.*

Your Turn Write each sentence in the past tense. Use the correct form of the verb in ( ).

1. The coach (shout) at us.
2. We (stop) what we were doing.
3. The coach (dare) us to run another mile.

Future-Tense Verbs

Future-tense verbs tell about action that is going to happen. Use the verb *will* to write about the future.

Next year, my family <u>will visit</u> our relatives.

Your Turn Write each sentence in the future tense. Use the correct form of each verb in ( ).

1. We (drive) over five hundred miles.
2. My grandparents (be) happy to see us.
3. I (write) letters to all my friends.
4. We (call) each other when we can.
5. I (start) a journal and (take) many pictures.

Subject-Verb Agreement

A **subject** and **verb** must agree. Add *-s* or *-es* only if the subject tells about one person or thing in the present tense.

My <u>mother calls</u> us, and <u>we come</u> right away.

Your Turn Write each sentence. Use the correct form of each verb in ( ).

1. The hikers (climb) the mountain.
2. The guide (choose) a spot for the tent.
3. The group (rest) for a while.
4. The cook (start) a fire and (make) dinner.
5. Last year, they (camp) here as well.

Verbs

The Verb *Have*

Use **have** with most subjects in the present tense.
For one person or thing, use **has**.
Use **had** for the past tense.

> *I <u>have</u> a red shirt. The girl <u>has</u> a blue shirt. We both <u>had</u> black shoes.*

Your Turn Write each sentence. Use the correct form of the verb *have*.

1. My mother (have) a question.
2. I (have) the answer.
3. Last fall, my sisters (have) a contest.

The Verb *Be*

For the present tense, use **is** if the subject is singular. Use **am** if the subject is *I*. Use **are** if the subject is plural or *you*.

For the past tense, use **was** if the subject is singular or *I*. Use **were** if the subject is plural or *you*.

> *Ann <u>is</u> the leader this year, but I <u>was</u> leader last year.*

Your Turn Write each sentence. Use the correct form of the verb *be*.

1. I (is) at the library.
2. You (is) at school.
3. Yesterday, Dad (is) at home.
4. Last week, we (is) all on vacation.

Contractions with *Not*

A **contraction** is a short form of two words. An **apostrophe** shows where one or more letters have been left out. Two irregular contractions are **can't** (can not) and **won't** (will not).

This <u>isn't</u> easy. You <u>aren't</u> ready. They <u>don't</u> want to go.

Your Turn Write each sentence. Form a contraction using the words in ( ).

1. My friend (did not) read the book.
2. The questions (are not) difficult.
3. Our teacher (does not) give us much time.
4. We (will not) finish before lunch.

Helping Verbs

A **helping verb** helps another verb show action. *Am, is* and *are* can help tell about action in the present. *Has* and *had* can help tell about action in the past.

Jess <u>is</u> telling a story. We <u>had</u> heard it before.

Your Turn Write each sentence. Underline the helping verb.

1. The boy is building a fort.
2. His father has helped him in the past.
3. We are watching them raise the roof.
4. Now I am bringing them lunch.

Verbs

Irregular Verbs

An **irregular verb** has a special spelling to show the past tense. Some also have a special spelling when used with the helping verb *have*.

Present	Past
come	came
do	did
eat	ate
give	gave
go	went
hide	hid
run	ran
say	said
see	saw
sing	sang
sit	sat
take	took
tell	told
write	wrote

Your Turn Write each sentence in the past tense. Use the correct form of the verb in ( ).

1. My friends (come) to my house yesterday.
2. Last weekend they (run) a race.
3. I (see) them training.
4. My friends (say) they would win.
5. They (go) fast and (do) well.

Combining Sentences: Verbs

When two sentences have the same subject, you can use the word **and** to combine the predicates.

Taylor swings the bat. _Taylor_ hits the ball.

Taylor swings the bat _and_ hits the ball.

Your Turn Use *and* to combine each pair of sentences. Write the new sentence.

1. My dad sings. My dad dances.
2. Paul claps. Paul stomps his feet.
3. Mother plays piano. Mother hums.
4. Jean is tired. Jean sits down.
5. We are having fun. We don't want to stop.

Pronouns

Pronouns: *I, You, He, She, It, We, They*

A **pronoun** takes the place of one or more nouns. The pronouns *I, you, he, she, it, we,* and *they* can be used as subjects in a sentence.

I like to ski. You and he like to surf.

Your Turn Write each sentence. Replace the underline word or words with a pronoun.

1. My friend lives near the beach.
2. The house is very small.
3. Mom has a sailboat.
4. My friend and I like to swim.
5. Are his brother and sister good swimmers, too?

Pronouns: *Me, You, Him, Her, It, Us, Them*

Some **pronouns** come after the verb in a sentence. The pronouns *me, you, him, her, it, us,* and *them* can be used in the predicate of a sentence.

Dad gave him the pen. He used it to write a poem.

Your Turn Write each sentence. Replace the underlined word or words with a pronoun.

1. We held the fair outside.
2. The rain soaked the boys and girls.
3. Who gave my sister an umbrella?
4. I saw my father inside his car.
5. An oak tree kept my friend and me dry.

Pronouns with *-self* and *-selves*

Some pronouns in the predicate tell about an action that a subject does for or to itself. The ending *-self* is used for singular pronouns. The ending *-selves* is used for plural pronouns.

The boy made <u>himself</u> a snack. We gave <u>ourselves</u> a pear.

Your Turn Write each sentence. Replace the word or words in ( ) with a pronoun.

1. My brother teaches (my brother) Spanish.
2. My mother asks (my mother) a question.
3. Could my parents teach (my parents) French?
4. The computer shuts (the computer) off.

Possessive Pronouns

A **possessive pronoun** takes the place of a possessive noun. It shows who or what owns something. *My, your, her, his, its, our,* and *their* are possessive pronouns.

I gave <u>my</u> homework to <u>our</u> teacher.

Your Turn Write each sentence. Replace the underlined words with a possessive pronoun.

1. <u>My sister's</u> room faces east.
2. She can see <u>the school's</u> playground.
3. <u>The building's</u> walls are made of brick.
4. <u>The teacher's</u> cars are parked nearby.
5. <u>My sister's and my</u> walk to school is short.

Pronouns

Pronoun-Verb Agreement

The verb of a sentence must agree with the pronoun that is the subject of the verb.

She laughs while _we perform_ our play.

Your Turn **Write each sentence. Use the correct present-tense form of the verb in ( ).**

1. She (draw) a map.
2. It (show) how to get to the lake.
3. We (hope) to get there by noon.
4. They (think) we may be lost.
5. Where (do) she think she is going?

Contractions

A **contraction** can be the short form of a pronoun combined with a verb. An **apostrophe** takes the place of the letters that are left out.

I'm sorry that <u>you'll</u> miss class today.

Your Turn **Write each sentence. Replace the underlined contraction with a pronoun and a verb.**

1. <u>He's</u> worried about the sick dog.
2. <u>We're</u> about to call the doctor.
3. Do you think <u>she'll</u> be able to help?
4. We hope <u>it's</u> not serious.
5. <u>You'll</u> soon feel better than ever!

Adjectives

Adjectives

An **adjective** is a word that describes a noun. Some adjectives tell what **kind** or how **many**.

Three dogs with <u>red</u> collars ran down the <u>dark</u> street.

Your Turn Write each sentence. Circle each adjective and underline the noun being described.

1. We'll need four apples for the pie.
2. Bake it for sixty minutes.
3. I prefer a thin crust.
4. Don't touch the hot plate!
5. Could I become a famous chef?

Articles

The words *the, a,* and *an* are special adjectives called **articles**. Use *a* before words that begin with consonant sounds. Use *an* before words that begin with vowel sounds.

<u>An</u> owl built <u>the</u> nest high in <u>a</u> tree.

Your Turn Write each sentence. Circle the articles.

1. A fox ran through our yard.
2. It woke up the dog.
3. I turned on a light outside.
4. A pair of eyes glowed in the dark.
5. I shut off the light in an instant.

This, That, These, and Those

This, that, these, and *those* are special adjectives that tell how many and how close. **This** and **that** refer to singular nouns. **These** and **those** refer to plural nouns.

> *I will read <u>these</u> books in my arms before I read <u>those</u> books on the shelf.*

Your Turn **Write each sentence. Choose the correct adjective in ( ) to complete the sentence.**

1. My sister enjoys (this, these) movie.
2. I like (that, those) actors.
3. (This, These) special effects are great.
4. (That, Those) monster scared me.
5. I would watch (these, this) movie again.

Adjectives That Compare

Add **-er** to an adjective to compare two nouns. Add **-est** to compare more than two nouns.

> *Bill is <u>taller</u> than me, but Steve is my <u>tallest</u> brother.*

Your Turn **Write each sentence. Add *-er* or *-est* to the adjective in ( ).**

1. My mom wants a (fast) car than our old one.
2. She looks at the (new) model of all the cars.
3. Does this car have a (high) price than that one?
4. This was the (hard) decision we've ever made!
5. Is one car is (safe) than another?

Adverbs and Prepositional Phrases

Adverbs

An **adverb** is a word that tells more about a verb. Adverbs tell *how, when,* or *where.* Many adverbs end in *-ly. We ran <u>quickly</u> to the front of the line.*

Your Turn Write each sentence. Circle each adverb. Then underline the verb it tells about.

1. I listened closely to the news.
2. The storm moved slowly out to sea.
3. We walked outside to check the sky.

Prepositional Phrases

A **preposition** comes before a noun or a pronoun. Together they make a **prepositional phrase**. Common prepositions include *in, at, of, from, with, to,* and *by.* A prepositional phrase can work as an adjective or an adverb that tells *how, when,* or *where.*

We ran quickly <u>to the front</u> <u>of the line</u>.

Your Turn Write each sentence. Underline the prepositional phrase. Circle the preposition.

1. I walked to the park.
2. Did you go with your friends?
3. We helped put trash in bags.
4. We did something good for our community.

Abbreviations

An **abbreviation** is a short form of a word. It usually ends with a period.

Main Street	Main St.
Lincoln Road	Lincoln Rd.
North Avenue	North Ave.
Apartment 6B	Apt. 6B
Mount Olympus	Mt. Olympus

Your Turn Write each address using an abbreviation.

1. 32 Front Street
2. 291 Jefferson Avenue
3. 7 Old Mill Road
4. Apartment 8H
5. 96 Mount Shasta Avenue

Titles

The abbreviation of a **title** before a name begins with a capital letter and ends with a period. Common titles before names are Mr., Ms., Mrs., and Dr.

Ms. Choi invited Dr. Shaw and Mr. Howe to the show.

Your Turn Write each name and abbreviation correctly.

1. ms. Ellen Daly
2. Mr Mark Bryant
3. dr denise Putnam
4. mrs. june lee

Mechanics: Abbreviations

Days of the Week/Months of the Year

When you abbreviate the days of the week or the months of the year, begin with a capital letter and end with a period. Do not abbreviate *May, June,* or *July.*

Sun.   Mon.   Tues.   Wed.   Thurs.   Fri.   Sat.

Jan. Feb. Mar. Apr. Aug. Sept. Oct. Nov. Dec.

Your Turn **Write each sentence with the correct abbreviation.**

1. Our first meeting was on January 23, 2005.
2. The report is due on November 5.
3. Can you come to a party on April 17?
4. No one likes to meet on Saturday or Sunday.
5. We will meet again on Thursday, March 12.

States

When you write an address, you may use United States Postal Service abbreviations for the names of states. The abbreviations are two capital letters with no period at the end.

Alabama	AL	Kentucky	KY	Ohio	OH
Alaska	AK	Louisiana	LA	Oklahoma	OK
Arizona	AZ	Maine	ME	Oregon	OR
Arkansas	AR	Maryland	MD	Pennsylvania	PA
California	CA	Massachusetts	MA	Rhode Island	RI
Colorado	CO	Michigan	MI	South Carolina	SC
Connecticut	CT	Minnesota	MN	South Dakota	SD
Delaware	DE	Mississippi	MS	Tennessee	TN
District of Columbia	DC	Missouri	MO	Texas	TX
		Montana	MT	Utah	UT
Florida	FL	Nebraska	NE	Vermont	VT
Georgia	GA	Nevada	NV	Virginia	VA
Hawaii	HI	New Hampshire	NH	Washington	WA
Idaho	ID	New Jersey	NJ	West Virginia	WV
Illinois	IL	New Mexico	NM	Wisconsin	WI
Indiana	IN	New York	NY	Wyoming	WY
Iowa	IA	North Carolina	NC		
Kansas	KS	North Dakota	ND		

Your Turn Write the U.S. Postal Service Abbreviation for each of the following.

1. Chicago, Illinois
2. Dallas, Texas
3. Miami, Florida
4. Los Angeles, California

Mechanics: Capitalization

First Word in a Sentence

The first word in a sentence begins with a capital letter. A **quotation** is the exact words of a person speaking. The first word in a quotation begins with a capital letter.

<u>O</u>ur teacher said, "<u>R</u>emember to pack up your books."

Your Turn Write each sentence. Use capital letters correctly.

1. our coach talked to the team.
2. he said, "keep your eyes on the ball."
3. I asked, "can we practice our kicking?"

Letters

All of the words in a letter's greeting begin with a capital letter. Only the first word in the closing of a letter begins with a capital letter. Use a comma after the greeting and closing of a friendly letter.

Dear Sir,   *Yours truly,*

Your Turn Write each part of a letter with the correct capitalization.

1. dear mr. holland,
2. sincerely yours,
3. dear dr. andrews,
4. best wishes,

Names and Titles of People

The names of people begin with a capital letter. Titles begin with a capital letter. Always write the pronoun *I* as a capital letter.

Mrs. Walker and I built a bird feeder.

Your Turn **Write each sentence. Use capital letters correctly.**

1. Mr. taylor agreed to be our tour guide.
2. i think mrs. Shea is a better choice.
3. She knows dr. Peter miller.

Names of Places and Geographic Names

The names of streets, buildings, cities, and states begin with a capital letter. The names of rivers, mountains, countries, continents, and planets begin with a capital letter.

You can view Mars at Mount Evans Observatory in Colorado.

Your Turn **Write each sentence. Use capital letters correctly.**

1. We drive to washington to see the columbia river.
2. The river runs between portland and vancouver.
3. We may also visit mount st. helens.

Mechanics: Capitalization

More Proper Nouns and Adjectives

The names of schools, clubs, teams, and businesses begin with a capital letter. The names of products begin with a capital letter.

The Elmwood School Ramblers sell their Healthy Serving snacks at the bake sale.

The days of the week, months of the year, and holidays begin with a capital letter. The names of the seasons do not begin with a capital letter.

Labor Day is the first Monday in September.

Most abbreviations begin with a capital letter.

Mr. Ellis spoke with Dr. Garcia about his illness.

The first, last, and most important words in the title of a book, poem, song, story, play, movie, magazine, or newspaper begin with capital letters.

My father reads the New York Times while I watch Alice in Wonderland.

Your Turn Write each sentence. Use capital letters correctly.

1. This year february begins on a friday.
2. How will ms. davis celebrate valentine's day?
3. The mill river band is performing today.
4. The concert began with "america the beautiful."

End Marks

A **statement** is a sentence that tells a complete thought. It ends with a **period (.)**.

A **question** is a sentence that asks something. It ends with a **question mark (?)**.

A **command** is a sentence that tells someone to do something. It ends with a **period (.)**.

An **exclamation** is a sentence that shows strong feeling. It ends with an **exclamation mark (!)**.

Do you like black beans? They are my absolute favorite! I like them with rice.

Your Turn **Write each sentence. Add the correct end mark.**

1. We can make soup for lunch
2. Do we have enough vegetables
3. This soup will be the best ever

Periods

Use a period to show the end of an abbreviation. Use a period with initials that stand for a person's name.

On Oct. 23, Bill loaned me a book by C. S. Lewis.

Your Turn **Write each sentence. Use periods correctly.**

1. Mr Greco and his son joined us.
2. My mother read a book by j d salinger.
3. Oct and Nov are the best months to visit.

Mechanics: Punctuation

Commas

Use a **comma (,)** between the names of cities and states.

Austin, Texas   Albany, New York   Boston, Mass.

Use a **comma** between the day and the year in dates.

June 5, 1977   Sept. 18, 2010

Use a **comma** after the greeting and closing in a friendly letter.

Dear Grandma,   Best wishes,

Use **commas** to separate words in a series.

She took pictures of the alligators, otters, and parrots.

Use a **comma** after the words *yes* or *no* or the name of a person being spoken to.

Yes, I know Ben. Tracy, have you met him?

Use a **comma** after a sequence word.

First, we walk. Next, we take the bus.

Your Turn Write each sentence. Add commas where needed.

1. Dear Aunt Polly
2. I hope you like living in Portland Maine.
3. Were you born on July 4 1976?
4. Do you like parades picnics and fireworks?

Apostrophes

Use an **apostrophe (')** with a noun to show possession. Use an apostrophe in a contraction to show where a letter or letters are missing.

My brother's cat won't come in from the rain.

Your Turn **Write each sentence. Add apostrophes where needed.**

1. Our familys pets had a bad day.
2. The cats tail got stuck in the door.
3. Our dogs cant find their toys.
4. The door on the birds cage wont open.
5. Youll have to bring it to Mr. Swansons shop.

Quotation Marks

Use quotation marks at the beginning and at the end of the exact words a person says.

My uncle asked, "Where is your bike?"

"I left it at the shop," I replied.

Your Turn **Write each sentence. Add quotation marks where needed.**

1. My sister said, Your tire is flat.
2. I ran over some rocks, I replied.
3. She asked, What will you do now?
4. I need to get home right now! I exclaimed.
5. Can I borrow yours? I asked.

Mechanics: Punctuation

Italics or Underlining

Use italics or an underline for the title of a book, movie, magazine, or newspaper.

<u>James and the Giant Peach</u>   *Dolphin Tale*

Your Turn **Write each sentence. Use italics or underline the titles.**

1. I read the book My Side of the Mountain.
2. The magazine Film Fun said it was also a movie.
3. "Was it as good as The Incredible Journey?" you asked.
4. The Santa Monica Herald didn't think so.
5. Let's watch Finding Nemo again tonight.